MW00799923

First Impressions

True Tales from the Road

By

Gare Allen

First Impressions. *Copyright 2015 by Gare Allen. All rights reserved. No part of this book may be used or reproduced in any manner without written permission from the author.*

This is a true story, however many of the names have been changed or omitted. Any resemblances to actual places, people (living or dead), or incidents that happened that are not listed are purely coincidental.

Also by Gare Allen:

The 7 Novellas Series: 7 Short Stories of

Reincarnation and Paranormal Experiences (based

on actual events)

7 Sessions-Book One

7 Regressions-Book Two

7 Apparitions-Book Three

7 Abductions-Book Four

7 Projections-Book Five

7 Predictions-Book Six

7 Reflections-Book Seven

and

The Dead: A True Paranormal Story

Chapter One

I observed a homeless man one afternoon outside of a grocery store. His appearance suggested that he had been living on the street for quite some time. He wore tattered and dirty clothing that, while baggy, was most likely form-fitting before the inevitable weight loss from a lack of food. I peered into eyes that reminded me of a scared dog, both cautious and hopeful as they stole quick glances through his long, grey, tangled hair. His sun-darkened skin was soiled with dirt and he smelled of sweat and body odor. My first impression was that the man had succumbed to an addiction that resulted in the loss of income and he sadly had no family or friends available for support. I think many would agree that it's unfair and unwise to presume someone else's story through the narrow lens of a first impression. However, as human beings, our curiosity often begs for this type of short-sighted speculation.

I promise you that my curious interest in the gentleman sitting on the concrete in the hot, Florida sun was anything but judgmental. In fact, my ability to recognize his heavy stare of worry, stress and a wary need for assistance, demonstrates my own experience with which, to a lesser degree, I can relate.

After my quick assessment of the man outside of the store, I proceeded inside to shop for groceries. Before hitting the aisles and armed with the, thus far, delusional expectation of winning the lottery, I stood in a lengthy line to purchase my weekly ticket. As I waited, I turned to see that the homeless man had made his way into the store and was asking a cashier to evenly exchange his coins for cash. An older, well-dressed man standing in front of me caught my line of sight and a conversation ensued.

"That guy is amazing." He said to me.

I could see that he was clearly looking at the homeless man as he spoke. His inflection failed to clearly define his use of the word, amazing, so I asked in response, "Amazing, in a good way?"

"Yes." The older man then explained his comment. "I used to see that guy in Starbucks every morning. I watched him read The New York Times and The Washington Post from front to back." I felt his actions were just slightly more 'amateur private eye' than 'creepy stalker' so I listened as he continued. "I started having conversations with him one morning. He could speak to economics, politics, world relations and any other subject I brought up. When he talks, he sounds like a professor at a university. Hell, I learned things from him and I have a master's degree in Economics."

I turned back and looked at the man with the torn clothing and dirty, weathered face accepting paper money in exchange for his quarters, nickels and dimes. Admittedly, I was surprised to find out that he was a bright, well-spoken and whether by an institution or self-learned, apparently thoroughly educated on several subjects. As I watched him place his money in his pocket, he looked up. His dim, sorrowful eyes were now alive with an exaggerated excitement and he quickly exited the store.

The older man spoke one last time after watching the homeless man leave. "I tried to give him some money once but he wouldn't accept it. It looks like he found some change on the ground and he's headed back to Starbucks. He's happy."

Having purchased his lottery ticket, the older man left and I handed the cashier my lotto card to scan. I hope I thanked her after she handed me my ticket but I honestly don't recall as my thoughts were still consumed with my new perception and moreover, the previous life occurrences of the homeless gentleman that produced his current circumstances.

We all have a story. The particulars of setting, character motivation and endgame can change with each passing moment as we encounter new experiences, obstacles, opportunities and, of course, the people that waft in and out of our lives. From the outside, one might observe a condition of life where these environmental elements act as bumper guards to maneuver us through our days; navigated down the, hopefully, chosen path in front of us.

From an early age the question is posed to us: what do you want to be when you grow up? With little life experience to draw from, we struggle to choose an informed or truly impassioned vocation. Hence, the responses that often include an astronaut and a cowboy. Don't get me wrong; those are courageous, valuable and respectable professions. Still, they are chosen from a child's fantasy laden imagination as opposed to a deep interest in aeronautics or maintaining the proud, family farm.

Most parents don't expect their child to know early on exactly to what profession or in which direction their life will lead them. They understand that their child's continuing life experiences will mold their personality. As they determine their likes and dislikes along with their interests and passions, they will eventually settle on a vocational course.

I think many of us would love to visit our past selves. If for no other reason than to see the incredulous expression on our past faces when we inform them of who and what we have become...and are still becoming. Indeed, we never stop growing in all of our roles that may include husband, wife, partner, father, mother, son, daughter, student, teacher, manager, trainer, and counselor and, well, the list goes on.

At some point we begin to find ourselves in various situations in which we are tasked with summarizing our personal, ongoing tale into a short dissertation that, hopefully, sums up our lives and describes the person that we are or are trying to be.

One moment where such an explanation may be warranted is during a party when introduced to strangers or, as some see them, potential new friends. Also, a successful job interview is contingent on our ability to convey a short and concise summary of who we are at that moment and confidently sandwich that between who we were and who we want to be, in relation to the job for which we are applying. Couple that pressure with the fact that multiple people are interviewing for the same position and writing the back of your baseball card becomes a much more monumental task. We do our best to express and communicate a clear picture of how we define ourselves but ultimately, we cannot truly control how we are perceived by others.

An impression is loosely defined as the first and immediate effect of an experience or perception upon the mind. Think back to your last interview, first date or when you simply met someone for the first time. Do you recall your very first impression of that individual? Aside from physical appearance and greeting, most of us would remember an instinctual emotional reaction. We either felt comfortable or threatened due to physical stature. Perhaps they were overly friendly which instilled comfort or, alternately, put us on edge while anticipating a false and forced personality fueled by an insecure need for approval. Regardless of how sure we are of our initial personality assessment, it will take the exchange of personal statistics such as our geographical residences, field of work or study, extracurricular hobbies and activities and countless other bits of personal information, to know if our first impression was accurate.

I discovered that uncovering someone's story is most easily obtained by simply engaging in casual conversation.

Chapter Two

A layoff from my now former place of employment of almost twelve years in mid-2014 afforded me the opportunity to focus on writing. By December of 2015, I had completed and self-published a series of seven metaphysical and paranormal short stories called *The 7 Novellas Series* which were inspired by paranormal events that had occurred in my life. A few months later I completed *The Dead: A True Paranormal Story* which describes, in detail, my real life supernatural and paranormal experiences that were weaved throughout the novellas.

While I wrote, I supplemented my income by driving for a ride sharing company. The application process was fairly simple. I applied online and submitted proof of car ownership, insurance and a valid driver's license. The company performed a background check, both criminal and driving, and after I shadowed a fellow employee on a ride, I was free to work as much or as little as I pleased. In my experience, ride sharing presents itself as a safe and pleasant alternative to the typical taxi experience.

I simply opened the app on my phone and awaited requests for rides. I then picked up the passengers and drove them to their desired destinations and repeated as necessary. They paid through the app and I received weekly deposits, sans the company's a twenty percent take. Using a scale of one to five stars, both the driver and the passenger rated and, if desired, commented on one another after each trip. A five star rating instills confidence in each other and makes for a more relaxed trip. The company's guidelines are such that if your rating is below four stars, you are terminated.

In addition to the star rating system, the app also provided a picture of the passenger to assist the driver with finding them in the event that they are with crowds of people. I admit that the picture, much like a dating site, provides an instant impression, albeit superficial, of that person's story.

Most of the people that I drove were very friendly and talkative. In fact, they often took the initiative and engaged me in conversation; asking me where I was from and how long I had been driving. Since my road warrior career was very short, I spoke, briefly, of my former job but mostly about my writing. Once I opened up about pursuing my passion for prose, and apparently alliteration, they reciprocated, in abundance.

I admit that the vast majority of my initial impressions and opinions, based on looks and greeting alone, turn out to be largely inaccurate. Similar to a job interview or a speed-date exchange, many passengers used the fifteen to twenty minutes available during their transport to inform me of their current social and professional status, general attitudes and personal goals. With nothing else to do but drive, I listened to their tales.

My very first fare was a young student at the local college. I picked him up on a Sunday afternoon in front of his dorm to drive him to his friend's apartment. He was a typical, thin hipster with dark skin and hair and carried a book-bag in one hand and his phone in the other. He barely uttered, "Hey" as he assumed his spot in the backseat.

As we drove, I felt compelled to be friendly to ensure that he would later grant me my first five-star review.

"How is your Sunday going?" I asked.

"Good." He replied without lifting his head up from his deep connection with his phone.

"What are your plans for the day?" I asked in hopes of opening up a line of communication.

"Study." He replied, still very much engaged with what I assumed was his Facebook wall.

It struck me as odd that he would be spending a warm, beautiful, Sunday afternoon studying inside.

I took one more shot at a conversation and asked, "What are you studying at school?"

The young man suddenly engaged me. He lifted his head from his phone and in an excited and elevated voice replied, "I'm studying physical therapy. I'm going to be a Physical Therapist!"

He's alive!

The student explained his choice of study without further prompt. "My mother had a stroke and it was a long, hard recovery for her. The therapists who worked with her were amazing. Without them, I don't think she would have recovered as well as she did."

I watched his face in the rearview mirror light up as he talked about his mother and her recovery from a devastating stroke. He became animated and demonstrative with broad smiles and hand gestures as he spoke.

He continued. "I want to help people. People who are recovering from strokes or injuries from accidents don't always have family to help them and they need someone who cares. I was too young to help my mom at the time of her stroke so those people were angels to us." He paused and looked out the window. "I want to help people."

I've endured over forty-six years on the planet and while still on this side of grumpy old man, I've certainly become more cynical. In an ignorant and small-minded moment I dismissed the young man as a student who was simply going through the motions of school with no focus, drive or direction. Why? Everyone has a story and everyone is writing their tale, fueled by their personal ambitions. Age, demeanor and looks are often a misleading cover depicted on their life's book and I know that. But, human nature sends our army of senses to assess and classify because we must immediately understand what we encounter to feel safe. That instinctive response is primal and varies in intensity with each individual but everyone wonders, even if they don't ask, as to the who, what, where and why. Especially, when we find ourselves in a strange place or in the company of a stranger.

Perhaps I needed to see the young man as witless and meek to ease the understandable fear of picking up strangers who, in some cases, sat behind you and in perfect striking position, had they carried a weapon with them. Some would see my emotional response as assuming the worst in others while I view it as being cautious and prepared.

Chapter Three

Not often enough, we are granted the opportunity to observe selfless kindness in the actions of loving and spirited people. During my second week of driving, I accepted a ride that was timed at sixteen minutes but would last almost an hour.

Responding to a pick-up request at a Wal-Mart, I arrived to find a middle aged man and woman waiting in front of the exit doors with two full shopping carts of purchased goods, a microwave oven and a dog. I pulled up close to the curb and recognized the vest resting on the back of a beautiful, black Lab. She was a seeing-eye dog.

My heart sank instantly. My thoughts and feelings rushed back to a time a few years prior when I lost my black Lab mix, Sobek, to cancer at the age of eleven and half years.

Back in early 2001, the company I worked for began to liquidate their stores. My position as District Manager was removed but luckily I was kept on to close the stores in my surrounding area. No longer required to drive out of state and spend countless nights away from home, I was finally able to adopt a puppy and provide it the time and care it required. I awoke one Saturday morning and made my way to the local shelter. As if ordering a number four combo in a drive-thru, I asked for a black Lab puppy. The woman arched an eyebrow and replied that I was in luck as a litter of eight pups, just two months old, had just been dropped off.

For the next eleven and a half years, Sobek spent many warm Florida days swimming in the pool in endless pursuit of a floating and mostly, indestructible dog toy. Tired from hours of swimming and playing, he slept at the foot of my bed, every night.

While my responsibilities as a driver included tasks specifically behind the wheel, my duties as a fellow human being to those who may require assistance knew few limits. I parked the car and greeted the couple. The intelligent Lab moved the woman to the car door and she very capably found the handle. I turned my attention to the man who seemed to have a similar sight disability but to a slightly lesser degree. Regardless, I assisted and placed the abundant bags of food and household items into my trunk. It took some time but the carts were emptied and I wedged the microwave oven behind my seat with the gentleman beside it.

Once back in the car, I found the woman seat-belted in the passenger seat with the black Lab at her feet; only her big, brown inquisitive Labrador eyes peering up at me.

Having worked in the pet industry, I knew the rules and so did the dog. While wearing the vest, she was working and was not to be approached or touched from anyone besides her handler. I therefor resisted my urge to reach out and scratch her adorable muzzle.

The woman began a direct, verbal exchange with the man in the backseat.

"Do you have the microwave?"

The man's arm was resting on the large metal oven as he replied. "Yup, right here."

"We got a good deal on the display model." The woman proudly bragged to me.

"Did you pick up the prescriptions?" The woman asked turning her attention back to her companion.

"Yes, all of them." He replied. In anticipation of her follow up question, he stated, "And, I confirmed our appointment with the doctor tomorrow at eleven a.m."

Satisfied that her mental checklist had been reviewed, the woman beamed a wide, pleased smile. "You take such good care of me."

The man nodded and countered with, "We take care of each other."

Despite their short conversation, their love was palpable. I instantly understood their strong commitment to one another as they worked together to ensure each other's well-being.

Directed by the GPS in my phone, I began the drive to the couple's home and couldn't help but recall Sobek as I glanced down at the loving, curious eyes of the dog. Without being asked, I told the woman about Sobek and my wonderful time with him. In response, she began to describe some of the service dogs that she had owned during her life. There may have been more, but she told me of four.

While it made sense after hearing it, I had not realized that the owners would keep the seeing-eye dogs after their service time had ended. Indeed, they are very much their pets, despite their servitude. I guess I assumed that they either were service dogs for their entire life or they went up for adoption after their service time ended; no longer of use to the individual in need of their assistance. My assumption was another limited, small-minded moment.

That's two, if you were counting.

Her lab remained still for the duration of the ride. I continued to resist the urge to rub that greying muzzle with my hand and respected the request clearly printed on her vest.

The woman described her past service dogs in fond reflection. Her first was also a Lab, but a yellow male called, Sammy. He had since passed away at the age of thirteen. Unfortunately, the bigger dogs often don't have the longevity of life that the smaller dogs possess. Next, was a small Samoyed mix called, Shadow. She described a fluff of hair atop short legs that she was told was white as snow. Her most recently retired dog was a Golden Retriever named Daisy. An extremely smart dog, she told me that Daisy would, without fail, anticipate her needs without command. Finally, she introduced the pooch at her feet, Sugar. At the mention of her name, her big, brown, expectant eyes turned to her handler and awaited direction.

During my almost twelve years in the pet industry, I learned a great deal about animal care. In fact, that was literally part of my position's title. The majority of the company's business was generated from the dog food and supplies departments. That dictated that the bulk of the internal training would be focused on canine care.

The best part of my job was touring stores and meeting the visiting pet parents and their canine companions. With three dogs of my own during my time in the industry, my heart carved a very large space for their well-being. Admittedly, I struggled with the use of dogs as service animals. On one side, I understood the benefit of their training and the use of their minds to mitigate the disability of their owner. In the case of my passenger, Sugar led her safely through crowded stores to deter her from tripping or walking into a display or other people. Sugar was very much her eyes and she trusted her implicitly.

Alternately, I wondered about the quality of life of a typical service-dog. Sugar was a healthy looking, two-year old Lab with a shiny coat and clean, white teeth. She appeared very well cared for, but what of her needs outside of her role? I had learned that dogs require more than just food and water. Exercise and socialization are paramount in fostering a happy, well-behaved and responsive pet. Additionally, we cannot forget the specific function of the domesticated breed that we, by design, instilled in them.

For example, while playing fetch with certain breeds is an hour or so of fun for us, it is behaviorally vital to those breeds named for that purpose. Sugar is a Labrador Retriever. Her very name defines her singular focus. Labs are social and loving and very much the perfect pack dog. They are too happy to be in charge and too big and strong to bring up the rear. Finding their comfort zone in the middle of the pack, they are known to thrive mentally and psychologically while in the frequent company of other dogs.

My personal opinions whirling through my mind ended when we arrived to the couple's home. I backed the car up to their door as instructed. The woman found her way out of my car and, with Sugar's direction, up the rock walkway to her front door. After shuffling his way along the same path, the man retrieved a rolling cart from inside the house and slowly wheeled it to the trunk. He filled it with his bags and my offer to carry the microwave oven inside was graciously accepted. I walked into their home and placed the oven on a kitchen counter top. The house was dark and I could barely see. All of the window treatments were closed but after a second or two, my brain understood the why.

I turned to say good-bye and found the woman standing beside her sofa with a broad smile on her face as she asked me if I would like to meet her pups.

Yes, please!

With one command, three dogs came running into the home from the opened backdoor. First was Shadow, the fluffy Samoyed mix. He found his way to me instantly and barked playfully at my feet. The Golden Retriever and Lab, Daisy and Sugar, entered as a pair. Sugar had apparently made quick use of the backyard for a bathroom break and was reunited with her retriever gal-pal. After a quick sniff around me they launched themselves into playful glee in the couple's living room. With her vest removed, Sugar was now off the clock and indulging her breed's social inclination to play with her fellow retriever. Big, healthy, active dog noises filled the house. The joy beamed from the woman's face as she listened to the soft, playful growls and howling barks of the dogs while they tussled about her living room.

It was abundantly clear that when they wore their vests, they intently, loyally and solely worked for her. The dogs provided her care and direction while ensuring safety and support. When the vests were removed, they were full throttle dogs. The woman fostered a loving home where the pups played and were well cared for in exchange for their love and support. Watching the woman beam with joy at the sounds of her playful pack, it was obvious that she loved them, whether they were at work or play.

I turned and noticed that the man was feeling his way through his kitchen as he put away the groceries. He carefully felt and identified each item and ran his fingers along the cabinets until he found its place. I observed that only the bottom shelves were utilized and the newly purchased, unopened boxes of food were placed behind opened ones.

The woman felt her way along the back of the couch until she found herself in front of the sofa and sat in what I assumed was her favorite and familiar spot. She raised both her arms and cupped her hands in front of her. I watched, unsure as to what she was doing. Within seconds, the man, smiling ear to ear, presented her with a hot cup of tea that he had warmed in the recently purchased microwave. The woman boasted a wide smile at retrieving her beverage and her glee illuminated the darkened room.

"Thank you, Sweetie." She sang as she smelled the aroma wafting from her cup.

"My pleasure, baby." The man replied and felt his way back to the kitchen to continue putting the groceries away.

I wondered how many times he had prepared for her a cup of tea. A hundred? A thousand? Yet, the act was still executed with his loving pleasure and she continued to find joy in a simple, hot drink.

It stood to reason that their quality of life and safety was dependent on routine regarding where they walk, sit and place their personal items. However, their care and love for each other and their pets demonstrated a deep affection that I believe was primarily performed out of love, rather than necessity.

Sugar broke free of the rough-housing long enough for me to finally scratch her slightly grey muzzle. I saw my own Lab in her big, brown eyes and my own watered at the overwhelming display of the couple's devotion to each other and the sweet, unconditional love and support of their dogs.

Chapter Four

A few weeks later on a sunny Sunday morning, I responded to a ride request, just a mile away. I arrived to the destination to find a very attractive, young woman waiting outside of her apartment. She had long, brown hair and soft green eyes. Maybe twenty-two years old, her toned, brown legs stretched out from her beige, tight shorts while her tan arms fell down beside a white, spaghetti-strap top.

Surprisingly, she climbed into the front passenger seat. I greeted her and after entering the destination's address into my phone's GPS, I asked what the day held in store for her. When she responded, I swear I heard the song *Valley Girl* by Frank Zappa in the background.

"Sunday fun-day with my BFF at her pool. It's gonna be totes fun."

Like many people, I sometimes allow my insecurities to rear their ugly head and I resent attractive people who also, in my opinion, unfairly boast a high intelligence in addition to their good looks. I honestly didn't see any reason to dislike her.

She posed the usual question about how long I had been driving. I replied with a vague response that included the words, "not long" and quickly professed my status as a writer.

The very pretty, young woman's response shattered my preconceived notions.

"You're a writer? That's awesome. I just finished *The Gift* by Nabokov."

My mind quickly accessed my literary files. "The *Lolita* author?"

She became excited. "Yeah! Did you read it?"

While I think I frowned, I'm certain I spoke low and under my breath as I replied. "Uh, no. I saw the movie, though."

Considering the multitude of smartass responses that she could have made, her reply was actually polite, if not short. "Oh."

I made a quick connection which I hoped would deliver some redemption as a self-professed writer. "So, being a fan of Nabokov, are you of Russian descent?"

She turned quickly and excitedly at my determination. "Yeah, I am. You put that together. Cool."

I suddenly felt like I deserved a treat or pat on the head.

"So, what genre do you write?" She asked.

"Metaphysical and paranormal." I replied.

She smiled and slowly nodded her head while she determined, "Oh, so you're one of those existential people."

I've been called worse.

"Who are some of your favorite authors?" I asked.

"Oh my God, I've read all of Kathy Reichs' books." She replied.

Knowing that the television show *Bones* was based on Reichs' writing, I quickly joked, "I bet they're better than the TV show."

She laughed. "Def!"

I took a guess as to her specific interests based on the book's content. "What sparked the interest in forensics?"

"Like, that's my major."

She went on to explain her insane schedule that included five days of classes, five days or rather, nights of restaurant serving; all while her car is in the shop in need of costly repair. Sunday is the only day that she gets to "decompress".

Her words brought us to the end of our short trip to her bestie's house. As she gathered her bag filled with swimming necessities, I wondered if Mattel had manufactured a "Smarty-Hottie-Forensics-Barbie". I felt like I had just met the live model.

Proving further that I should refrain from viewing people through a narrow lens, the young woman left me a five star rating along with a short comment describing me as, "gregarious, fun and professional."

As I drove away, my mind recalled a platitude in perception that states, "It's more important to hear what people say and not how they say it". While our conversation was casual, she was sharp and well-read. I'm sure I would have enjoyed a lengthy discussion on authors' styles and the motivation of her intrigue with forensics. I thought about the focus that a full class load warrants and how disciplined she would need to be to complete her work inside and outside of the classroom. Also, considering the forced pleasantries that servers must adopt to foster a positive dining experience and ensure a good tip, I would need a day to regenerate also. Indeed, today was not about school or work and she didn't need to put on any pretenses. It was Sunday-funday and she was simply being herself.

Chapter Five

My next notable passenger was picked up at his home in an older part of the city. I pulled up to a sturdy but faded red brick home with timeworn awnings above the windows. I watched as a very large man standing well over six feet tall and boasting a massive, muscular build ambled out of the front door. He wore white khaki shorts and a very tight, grey t-shirt. With the exception of his face above his jawline, he was covered in colored tattoos from his neck down to his feet.

Complete badass. I thought to myself.

I understand the dedication, discipline and devotion to a regimented weight-lifting program and consistent cardio. Even more vital is the strict, mundane diet that is truly the key to a chiseled physique. Judging by the man's mass, vascularity and presumed single-digit body mass, he is in a gym three to four hours a day and no less than six days a week.

While I stand five feet and eight inches and boast a solid build, I am nowhere near his size. However, to a lesser degree, I have lived, respected and enjoyed the weight-lifting lifestyle, sans the cardio. Additionally, I have three tattoos that are mostly out of view; discreetly above my elbows on both arms. I am itching to sleeve my arms with intricate ink and begin a massive tattoo on the broad canvas that is my back. Between you and me, it's a safe bet that an anticipated midlife crisis will pull the trigger on that desire in just a few years, when I turn fifty.

The bodybuilder opened the rear passenger door and leaned down before asking, "Is it alright if I bring my snake?"

I paused at his unexpected query. Before I could formulate a reply, my gaze fell to the reptile in question. Wrapped around his muscular, inked arm was a three and a half foot long, yellow, Burmese Python.

Once again, my time in the pet supply industry paid off with the ability to recognize and feel at ease when adjacent to what I knew to be a non-poisonous snake.

"All good." I finally replied.

The passenger had already entered his destination through the app's GPS. While it directed me towards the address, there wasn't a business name and I didn't recognize the street. He didn't have a gym bag, so I was mildly curious as to where this guy might be going at noon on a weekday afternoon, with a snake.

I employed my now standard, opening query that often triggered a continued dialogue that, at the time, I didn't realize would end up on these pages.

"What's on tap for the day?"

"Going to work." The big man replied.

Making what I thought was an obvious deduction, I asked, "Do you work for a pet store?"

The man looked confused for just a second and then glanced down at the snake and back to my eyes in the rearview mirror.

"No, I bring this guy with me for the kids." He then explained what occupied his time outside of the gym. "I work with homeless kids at a children's shelter."

My heart and head fell to the memory of my mother. As a young child, she had spent time in an orphanage before finding the loving support of a family unit with her foster parents. Once, she had described her experience in a children's home as less than pleasant and cited unforgivable treatment of her and the other orphans during the holidays.

On Christmas Eve, charitable organizations would deliver toys that they had collected through donation drives to the parentless boys and girls. For many of the orphans, the receiving of this gift was the only Christmas moment they would enjoy.

My mother told me that once the charity workers left, the staff in the home would collect the presents from the orphans and take them home to their own children.

Pushing aside the sad memory, I asked if I could hear more about the man's work at the children's home. He was more than happy to explain his responsibilities and moreover, his mission.

"I keep the kids in line and teach them responsibility." He said with a stern tone. "Most of them are really good kids. They just need guidance and a respect for rules. There's not enough room and it's always crowded so tensions are high. No one gets any privacy. It's a tough life." His voice softened slightly. "I want them all to succeed in life."

My mind recalled a tough soccer coach I had as a kid who was every bit a drill sergeant even when it wasn't warranted. The guy in the backseat had a physical presence and a deep voice that most assuredly commanded respect. I doubt he needed to yell to receive compliance and while his speech was direct and even, he seemed, so far, like a caring, decent guy.

Pulling on my previous vocation, I recalled the term I needed to answer the begging question of the cold-blooded snake adorning his thick forearm.

"Are you into Herpetology?"

I watched his face in my rearview mirror quickly change from confused to annoyed, so I quickly defined the term as the study of reptiles. His chuckle and sigh of relief along with his avoidance of my eyes in the mirror told me that those first four letters of the term I had uttered, "herp", had directed his mind to a very different and uncomfortable subject matter.

Still smiling at the misunderstanding, he explained the presence of the python. "B.P. here teaches the kids respect." He held up his arm and the snake lifted its head as if surveying its surroundings from a new vantage point. "Ya see, most people have a fear of snakes but not a lot of respect for them."

I silently agreed with the first assertion but wondered where he was going with the second statement. My secondary thoughts were trying to figure out what the initials, B.P. stood for. Sensing his desire to elaborate on a snake's requirement for respect, I prompted him to continue with a question.

"Do you mean respect of the snake for safety's sake?"

I could see his head shaking from side to side in the rearview mirror as he answered. "No. Fear of a snake keeps you safe from them, for the most part." He paused. I assumed it was more for

4

dramatic effect than to allow me to further entice an explanation from him so I remained quiet until he resumed his commentary.

"Each day, a different kid has to care for B.P. When they have him, they are completely responsible for his well-being. They hold him, protect him, clean his habitat and once a week, they feed him." He held up his left arm and pointed to the roof of the car. "If they can show respect for a snake, then they can respect anyone and anything. Respect is vital to fitting in and gaining friends." His face fell soft and his eyes darted away from my line of sight. "Most of these kids have no confidence and act out. They're seen as outsiders and usually don't have any friends at school. We all need the support of family and friends to be successful in life. They don't have any real family but I'm gonna make sure they are able to make friends."

I admired and respected the man's dedication to the well-being of the children under his care. The lesson of respect with regard to caring for a snake made sense to me. Many parents will purchase a hamster or a goldfish for a young child and teach them how to care and provide for it. The man's thought process of teaching valuable respect using the snake was an extension of that premise but with older children.

The GPS alerted me that we had arrived to the destination. Quickly, I asked the man what had led him to work with children in need.

As he exited the car, he smiled and replied, "The obvious answer."

Although I hadn't previously considered it as motivation, I inferred that he had grown up a parentless child. Before he could shut the door, I blurted out one last question. "What does B.P. stand for?"

His expression was a mixture of surprise and annoyance when he answered, "Burmese Python."

Now, *that* was obvious.

At first glance of the massively muscular and tattooed man holding a snake, I would not have guessed that he boasted such a background and honorable purpose in life. He may never hear a thank-you from the children when they achieve adulthood, raise a family and become productive members of society. As is the case with most of society's everyday heroes such as military personnel, policemen and women, firefighters and EMT's, his drive is a result of a passion for helping people, not a need for gratitude.

Chapter Six

Sometimes when meeting someone, I get an initial impression that is slightly more accurate than not. While not a frequent occurrence, it does happen. Such was the case when I arrived to pick up a young girl whom I will refer to as, Tania.

One early afternoon, I pulled up to a technical school and quickly identified a young girl with long, dark hair as my passenger. I waved at her and she acknowledged me with a wave back with one hand while the other pressed a phone against her left ear. While I waited for her to gather her belongings that were on the ground at her feet, I tapped the appropriate arrival button in the app and sent her destination to the GPS. When I looked back up, Tania was standing with her books, a large bag and her purse just a few feet from the car.

My first thought was to get out and open the door for her. I was raised in the South and still possess some chivalrous genes. Still very much engaged in her phone call, I tried to catch her eye but she was not looking in my direction. My second thought was that she wanted to finish her conversation in private which is why she hadn't gotten into the car, yet. So, I waited.

A moment later, she put her books and bag in the backseat and then proceeded to join me in the front. Tania spoke plainly and confidently as she informed me that we were going to a mall. What she didn't tell me was that I would be getting another lesson in respect.

Immediately after I began to drive off, she resumed the conversation on her phone and would remain engaged with several callers for the duration of the twenty-five minute trip. I wondered why she didn't sit in the backseat since she clearly favored her phone over a conversation with me. Instead, I would endure not only her side of the chat, but the muffled yet, unfortunately, mostly, discernable responses of the person at the other end of her call.

It was only a few minutes into the ride when I learned that she had been disrespected by a female acquaintance named Mina and had summarily deemed the friendship, over. I'm pretty sure she didn't take a breath during the first call that informed a currently approved friend of the atrocity committed by the now shunned friend.

Yes, the first of three calls, where she repeated the same story and, to her credit, mostly verbatim and without embellishment. With each conversation, the volume of her voice increased with seemingly no regard to my presence. Tania was resolute in her judgment and by the final call, had elevated the severity of Mina's act of contempt to that of a murder one charge.

So, what was the act of treachery? Mina decided to visit Tania's boyfriend, Romeo at his home while Tania was at school.

I'm not entirely sure Romeo was his given name. Tania repeatedly referred to him as "My Romeo", which could be her loving nickname for him and obviously an impassioned literary reference. I'm guessing she hasn't read the end of that story.

Now, and Tania was very clear on this point, she believes that Romeo and Mina did not engage in any kind of inappropriate activity whatsoever. She repeatedly announced, and I quote, "I trust my man and I know he would never do me wrong."

So, what was the issue? Tania felt that Mina's visit to Romeo at his home without her knowledge and what I assumed would also be her approval, was an unforgivable act of betrayal and disrespect.

A lengthy red light afforded me the opportunity to consider Tania's condemnation. If I was to visit the wife of a friend of mine in their home while he was away and he were to find out later that I had been there without his knowledge, I could see where he would experience several emotional reactions.

First, he would be surprised which, in this case, might make him feel left out and even deceived. Whether intentional or not, it's not a good feeling to be left in the dark. Next, his protective instincts would fuel a mixture of anger, disappointment and perhaps a touch of paranoia for drama's sake. He will accept nothing short of clear and concise answers as to why he wasn't told and the reason for the occurrence in the first place.

As I thought more about that scenario, there was really no reason I could conceive that would necessitate a visit to a friend's wife without him being informed. Furthermore, if a situation arose that warranted my visit to his home, I would ensure that he was involved in that decision, to Tania's point, simply out of respect.

So, why was Mina visiting Romeo? It turns out that Mina owns her own cleaning service and cleans their house every other week. She arrived to their home to complete the bimonthly maid service. For Tania, that was not an acceptable reason and certainly not a good excuse.

I learned Mina was aware that she was forbidden to visit when Tania was not home. Both me and the friend on the other end of the phone listened as Tania explained the contractual terms outlined in their agreement. According to Tania, Mina is paid sixty-five dollars to clean their home, twice a month. Their written contract stipulates that she is only to perform the service when Tania is home. The agreement specifically states that she is not to be alone in the house with Romeo for any reason.

It's here where I wondered why that stipulation would need to be included in the service contract. Apparently, the person on the other end of the phone was similarly curious because Tania explained its purpose.

After hearing the story a total of three times I was able to sort through the slang and obtain the facts. I'll translate:

"Her sister was all up in him before."

Mina's sister, Christina, had dated Romeo several years ago.

"She doesn't come around but I don't know what's up."

While the romance had been long over, Tania felt that Mina might be persuaded to allow Christina to accompany her to their home and put Romeo in an uncomfortable situation.

"He's sweet and he doesn't know about these bitches."

Tania feels Romeo is oblivious to continued adoration by countless women, including his ex-girlfriend, Christina.

She closed out the call with a fairly diva-esque statement, a la Aretha Franklin.

"All it is, I mean, all it is…is respect. That's all. She has no respect for me. It's all R-E-S-P-E-C-T."

As we arrived to the entrance of the mall, she concluded the third call with a similar spelled punctuation. Just before she hung up, she pulled the phone away from her ear to view the incoming call.

She then asked, with an exaggerated tone of disbelief, "Can you believe that bitch is calling me now?"

Tania exited the car and pulled her belongings from the backseat while holding the phone to her ear. As the backdoor shut, I found myself mildly curious as to Mina's side of the story. In all honesty, I had gotten sucked into the Jerry Springer-like drama and wanted to hear the big showdown between the squabbling parties.

The next morning I received my usual email that listed the previous day's fares, including tip amount, rating and comments. Tania had given me my first four-star rating, had opted to not include a tip with the fare and wrote the following comment:

"Good driver, but didn't open the door for me. A man should always open a door for a woman."

R-E-S-P-E-C-T, indeed.

Chapter Seven

My first passenger pick-up from the airport was a short, young man I found waiting with a black backpack and a skateboard. His initial overly enthusiastic greeting of "What's up, dude?" helped me to instantly categorize him as a typical "skater/surfer dude" type. I noted the rest of his appearance as he found his way into the backseat which included long, blond hair reaching down from under his brown cap to a layered torso of t-shirts and a hoodie. His attire begged for a comment.

"It's gonna be mid-80's all week." I informed him.

He immediately unzipped his hoodie to remove it as he replied. "Yeah, dude, it's hot here."

"Where are you from?"

"New York."

"Yeah, guess it's a little cooler there."

"For sure, dude."

I typed the destination into the GPS and began the short fifteen minute drive to the local university. Expecting small talk at best, I engaged my passenger in friendly dialogue in my continued effort to receive five-star ratings.

"What brings you to Florida?"

"Visiting a friend down here and going to a tournament this weekend."

"What kind of tournament?"

"The Tampa Pro Skateboarding Contest."

Thanks to an energy drink display in a convenient store I had recently seen, I was aware of the upcoming event.

"The *Red Bull* one?" I asked.

"Yeah, dude! It's gonna be awesome." He determined.

"What do you do in New York? Are you in school?" I asked.

"Yeah, I'm going to Cornell Veterinary College."

I was definitely surprised at his response given the seven to nine years required for such degrees. It wasn't my intention to sell this young man short, but an expensive trip to Florida for a skateboarding event suggested a different set of priorities. At least, that was my ugly snap-judgment of my passenger's convictions.

"That's a big commitment. What made you want to be a vet?" I asked.

I watched him respond in the rearview mirror. His clenched jaw and serious tone told me that I had hit an emotional nerve.

"My dad was a vet. I'm going to continue the family practice." He paused and nodded his head to the affirmative as if reassuring himself. The casual surfer tone and jargon was now replaced with a serious and scholarly delivery as he continued. "My dad was the most affordable vet in the area. Most people want to help their animals but sometimes they can't afford it. He always made sure they could treat their animals."

The past tense reference of his father as well as his solemn expression suggested that his dad had passed. I admired the young man for his desire to honor his father's work and continue the family business but kept that to myself in favor of lightening the mood.

"Do you have animals of your own?"

2

His smile returned. "Yeah, tons of dogs. Mostly Labs. What about you?"

"A couple of mixed breeds. A Chow/Akita and a Pit Mix. I lost my Lab/Rottweiler mix a few years ago when he was almost twelve."

So much for lightening the mood.

"What happened to the Lab/Rottie mix?"

My lip curled as I recalled the particulars of his diagnosis. "He had a bone cancer that attacked the left side of his skull." I explained.

Knowingly, he clarified, "It's called Osteosarcoma."

I remembered the term as he spoke it and nodded. "Yeah, that was it."

"That's definitely common for the breed…unfortunately." He stated.

The young man sounded like a second year vet student. As we arrived to the university, his thoughts must have fallen to his friend and the upcoming skateboarding event because his serious look was wiped clean with a happy smile.

"We're here. Have a great weekend. And, good luck at vet school."

"Thanks, dude!" With that, he had grabbed his bag and board and was out the door.

In high school, my friend base spanned many different cliques. Among them, the jocks, the popular kids, the stoners, the nerds and, my favorite, the skaters. For the record, I've always been a Trekker so the nerds were definitely a close second.

From my perspective, the skaters appeared to have a singular purpose in their young lives and that was to enjoy the thrill of the board. They possessed an endless drive to add one more flip or master another trick that defied gravity. Their insatiable need for high speed maneuvers kept them on shopping plaza walkways and sidewalks until the sun set or they were chased away by the mall or plaza's security guard.

They were always pleasant and happy, if not short on words. The skaters often kept to themselves and I never saw them fight. While I found their superficial, light-hearted vibe refreshing, it was difficult to really get to know any of them. As a result, they were assumed to be of average intelligence or less and not given much more consideration. That got me thinking about my friends from high school.

Thanks to Facebook, you can "catch up" with any of your old friends, and enemies for that matter, without even speaking to them. Their walls include photos, locations visited and, sometimes regrettably, personal opinions, attitudes and values communicated via memes, shared articles and late night, alcohol-fueled rants. The onslaught of personal information and insight quickly answers the question, "I wonder how he or she is doing?"

After recalling the names of three friendly skaters from yesteryear, I easily found them on Facebook and soaked in, among other things, their marital status, favorite restaurants and current vocations.

To my surprise, two of the three were still friends and active skateboarders. Additionally, they had added surfing, biking and several other outdoor sports to their list of passions. As I stalked, or rather, perused their wall, I discovered that they were business owners together. Their business model included extreme sports equipment rental and instructional lessons to enthusiasts and vacationers. Both were now married with children and seemed to have been lucky enough to parley their childhood passion into a means of living.

The third high school skater's wall informed me that he had become a software developer and was also married with children. However, as I continued to scroll through his online life, it was clear that not only had he not abandoned his passion for extreme sports, he was channeling it in a philanthropic endeavor.

The now grown skateboarder spent much of his free time working with children suffering from any number of physical ailments and muscular disorders to help them achieve their goal of simply riding a bike or a skateboard down a sidewalk.

Well done, skateboarder dude.

Chapter Eight

My perceptions widened, I had passed the point of beating myself up for stereotyping people based on looks and first impressions. I had moved on to a more satisfying endeavor of uncovering their personal, albeit abbreviated, story.

No one was more surprised by the interest I had developed in other people's background than me. I've never been a people person and have always kept a very small select group of friends in my inner circle. Many of my jobs dictated a strong level of communication and customer service and I ensured that I delivered on that requirement. However, it was hardly enjoyed.

Truth be told, if you aren't part of my club, find another hangout. Indeed, I always thought my welcome mat sent a mixed message.

Don't get me wrong, I don't hate people. I simply prefer quality over quantity. I'd rather interact with two or three amazingly interesting and entertaining individuals than socialize with dozens of people who don't spark my interest.

It's possible, ok, *highly* possible, that, in the past, I may have sold some people short before I had the chance to hear the particulars of their life's endeavors and what fuels their drive. Thus, I may have missed an opportunity to allow entry of another amazing individual into the club.

Shame on me.

Chapter Nine

Late on a Saturday morning, I picked up a passenger who would prove to be something very different from my initial assessment that was determined by my first impression.

After arriving to my pick-up address, I dialed the number for the passenger, Rose, to request assistance in gaining access through the locked, iron gates outside of her retirement center.

No answer. I tried twice more but she did not pick up her phone. A car honked behind me, apparently having grown impatient and desiring entry through the gates. I swung my car around and tailed the car inside.

I made my way down the long drive to the main entrance of the home. A grey-haired woman with bright yellow shorts and a matching tank top waved her arms at me as if assisting a landing plane. Her wide, floppy, straw hat remained on her head despite her wild movements.

Pulling up to the circular drive, I had barely stopped when she opened the passenger door and climbed inside.

"It's about time." She snarled.

Confused, I checked the app on my phone and noted the exact time it took for me to arrive was only eleven minutes. Before I could protest her comment, she dug an address out of her oversized bag and shoved it in front of my face. With it, came the assaulting stench of stale, cigarette smoke.

Tolerance of impolite people has never been in surplus where I was concerned. Nevertheless, I felt reasonably confident that I possessed enough patience to handle a surly, sixty-something year old woman in a southern woman's floppy hat.

The GPS told me that I would endure approximately thirty minutes with this already tense woman before we reached our destination. Not a big fan of overly dramatic or obnoxiously rude individuals, I took a deep breath and braced myself.

As I drove off, the older lady mumbled to herself, nervously. Although her utterings were mostly unintelligible, she seemed more anxious than angry. I waited until we had merged onto the interstate, where the majority of the ride would take place, to engage her in casual conversation.

"So, what are your plans for the day, ma'am?" I asked cautiously.

"Ma'am?" She scoffed. "This ain't a limo so you can drop the formalities." She softened slightly. "And, call me Rose."

Deadpan, droll and direct? Now, that I can deal with.

I held back my laughter. "Where are we headed, Rose?"

She whined a little as she answered. "Oh, my son sent you to bring me over to his house for my birthday."

Trying to keep it real and match her current mood, I said, "I'd wish you a happy birthday but I'm guessing you're not into it."

She seemed to appreciate my early understanding of her state of mind with regard to the planned celebration.

"No, not really." She raised her arm and gestured, with palm out, into the air in front of her. "He invited dozens of people that I barely know so it's going to be a big thing and, well, that's not really what I want."

"What would you rather be doing on your birthday?" I asked as if I had known this woman for much longer than a few minutes.

She held her hands together in her lap. "I just want a simple dinner with my son and my daughter."

"And, they would rather throw you a big party?" I asked.

"Well, my son would, yes." She paused and rummaged through her large bag. "Mind if I smoke?"

Politely, I replied, "Yes."

"Thanks." Rose proceeded to light her cigarette. Her first puff sent a cloud of smoke between us. In response, I cracked all four windows but remained silent.

To this day, I'm not sure if she misunderstood my "yes" as approval for her to light up or if she asked merely as a courtesy with no intention of honoring a denied response. Part of me was annoyed at her dismissal of my response while another part of me appreciated her decision to do whatever the hell she wanted to do. Ultimately, I decided that it was her birthday and if she wanted to smoke, so be it.

Rose fell quiet and stared out of the window at the road as she dragged on her cigarette. After she was done, she tossed it out the small space created by the cracked window. I rolled down all four windows for a few seconds to release the residually trapped smoke and then closed them. If she understood my reasoning, she never said.

She finally broke her silence with a surprising bit of information. "I'm seventy-five, you know."

I was floored. It was my understanding that smoking aged and wrinkled skin drastically. I had her estimated in the low sixties, sixty-five at best.

"You look amazing!" I blurted out.

Rose flashed the first smile of the trip. "Well, thank you."

Another lull ensued until I asked if she had any grandchildren.

"Oh, yes. I have six grandchildren. Four boys and two girls. But, most of them are away in school or busy with their lives. I won't see them today."

"It's nice that your kids live locally, yes?"

She was short. "My son does, yes."

"Have you always lived in Florida?" I asked.

Her voice elevated in volume and pitch. "Oh, yes. We lived in South Tampa for thirty-eight years. We had a big backyard with a pool. It was one of those small, above-ground pools, but the kids loved it. Especially, Anne." Her voice dropped back down to the deadpan and direct zone. "Until my husband ran off with another woman and left me so we had to sell the house. The kids were all grown by then so I ended up in the retirement home where I've been ever since."

I continued driving without comment. Rose became much more fidgety as we closed in on her son's house. We arrived to her son's driveway a few minutes before noon. Rose sat still and frowned at the single balloon tied to the mailbox and dancing in a light breeze.

Without taking her eyes off of it, she remarked, "Does he think I'm six years old?"

I officially liked Rose at this point.

In a soft tone, I smiled and spoke, "Well, Rose, as much as you might not want to hear it, I wish you a happy birthday."

Her gaze remained on the balloon on the mailbox as she answered. "Thank you." After a brief pause, she looked at her watch. "My son isn't expecting me until noon. Would you mind if I had one last cigarette before I go in there? He gives me such a hard time about it."

The heavy emotion in her voice was palpable and while I couldn't see her eyes, I was sure they were tearing.

"Sure." I rolled down the windows and turned off the car. As a small birthday gesture, I tapped the "arrived" button in the app so that the ride would not incur further charges.

She puffed in silence while turned away from me. Her sadness and anxiety seemed to surpass the annoyance of an unwanted party.

"Rose, are you alright?"

She nodded her head and wiped her eyes with her free hand. After one last, long drag on her cigarette, she tossed the butt out of the window and to the ground.

I exited the car and walked around to the passenger door where I opened it for her. As she stepped out, I could visibly see the tears I had suspected were falling down her cheeks.

"Rose, what is it?" I asked.

She forced a smile, held her hands over her heart and spoke through sobbing sadness.

"This is my first birthday without my daughter."

My mind recalled our short chats and the several mentions of her son but only brief references to her daughter.

"She passed a few months ago."

As if on instinct, I took Rose by the hand and began walking her up the driveway. Her son met us halfway to the door.

He gently took his mother's other hand in his own and wrapped his arm around her in a comforting embrace.

Her son nodded a gracious gesture my way and I respectfully left.

Once back on the interstate, I turned off my "driver available" status in favor of reflecting on Rose.

The reason for her sadness was evident and the large group of people waiting for her in her son's house explained her heightened level of anxiety. I recalled her answer as to how she wanted to spend her birthday.

"I just want a simple dinner with my son and my daughter."

The words hit me hard in the gut. I've felt the same sense of loss each birthday and holiday since my mother passed. The first year is definitely the worst so I feel for Rose with all of my heart.

Having studied, at length, how to deal with loss, I recognized her son's attempt to show support by providing a large gathering of people on her birthday. If all goes well, her spirits will be lifted by the outpouring of birthday wishes, gifts and general good will. The goal is to remain busy and immerse yourself in all of the love and support around you.

It's a sound concept but it leaves out one point. Later that night, when Rose is home alone, the reality and devastating loss of her daughter will find its way back into her heart. She will grieve, cry and miss her terribly; the day's events having merely delayed the inevitable.

Rose came across crass and rude at first impression. In hindsight, I believe her behavior was a defense mechanism against her true feelings of despair and sadness.

After meeting Rose, I felt a little guilty. Having grown up in Florida, I've come to dislike many of the countless grumpy old men and women that assume residence to escape the harsh winters of the north. I've never understood why people who no longer work and are free to golf and drink all day would be so miserably rude to those around them.

Going forward, I can safely assume that there's often a significant reason, of which I am unaware, for their behavior.

Chapter Ten

A response to a ride request early on a Friday night brought me to the apartment complex of two women. Both in their late thirties, they thanked me for picking them up as one climbed into the backseat after the other called "shotgun".

They had already keyed their destination into the app so I easily tapped my phone for directions and off we went.

As if full disclosure of their dynamic were merely a "hello", the short, red-haired woman in the front seat informed me that they were a couple. She introduced herself as Beth and her partner as Vanessa.

Vanessa waved somewhat nervously from the backseat and watched my eyes in the rearview mirror. She wore her dark brown hair in a long pony tail and boasted a bronze beach tan while Beth's skin was a contrasting Irish, pale white.

I found their openness refreshing and asked, "How long have you two been together?"

Vanessa proudly answered, "We just celebrated ten years."

Beth decided that in addition to their relationship status, I should be made aware of the reason for their ride today.

"We're going to see a specialist. Vanessa has some growths on her skin. Mostly, on her arms and legs. They're dark spots but some are almost black. Like tiny, ink blots."

Specific, very specific.

I caught Vanessa's annoyed eyes in the rearview mirror.

"I hope everything checks out ok." I told her.

She forced a smile and looked away, seemingly not pleased with Beth's offering of personal information and subsequently a little embarrassed at my sentiment. "Thanks. I'm sure they're nothing."

Beth turned to address her partner. "Me, too. But we need to make sure." She began to bite on an already short fingernail and spoke under her breath. "I always worry about you."

It was clear that Beth was very protective of her companion of over ten years. While I admired the genuine affection, I felt a lighter topic might make the drive more enjoyable. It had been my experience that I could bring a smile to any face when I prompted someone to discuss their children or pets. Given Florida's laws regarding adoption by gay couples, I made the assumption that they didn't have any children. That left pets as a cheerier topic of conversation.

Cats. If there was one stereotype that wouldn't let me down in a moment of limited thinking, it was that lesbians love their cats.

"We have two dogs."

Thanks a lot, small, stupid mind.

Vanessa found her voice and the energy inside the car changed dramatically. "We have a Chihuahua and a Maltese. Their names are Tito and Boston."

Boy dogs? I was batting zero.

"Boston's an interesting name." I said.

Both girls smiled and Beth continued to convey her relationship resume. "That's where we met. When we got our first place together, we adopted Boston. He's been with us ever since."

Luckily, Florida doesn't discriminate against same-sex parents of pets.

I shared the names of the many breeds that comprise my eclectic pack at home and flashed a few pictures at the next red light. Vanessa leaned up between the two front seats and gasped at the various mixing of a Chow Chow, Akita, Pit Bull, Lab, Great Dane and Hound Dog.

In an effort to keep the focus off of Vanessa's impending doctor's visit and on a lighter subject, I asked about their line of work. I will admit that I expected to hear titles such as manager, instructor or other authoritative positions.

Vanessa informed me that she worked as a dental assistant during the week and as a floral artist on the weekend for a large, online, flower supply company.

Her response was perhaps just slightly off-center of stereotype's target.

Beth then announced that she was a truck driver.

Bulls-eye.

I suddenly understood Beth's sense of urgency and her comment regarding her constant worry of Vanessa.

"Do you drive locally or across country?" I asked.

"Everywhere." She replied. "Even Canada."

"So, you're gone for long stretches?"

3

Vanessa's face flashed a frown and Beth's voice lowered as she spoke. "Yeah, for days and sometimes over a week at a time."

The girls fell quiet, seemingly lost in their respective thoughts. We drove in silence for a few minutes until Beth's worry got the best of her.

"Do you know anything about skin cancer?"

Vanessa's head swung to the left and away from the passing road that she had been so pensively watching. "Beth!"

She defended herself. "That's what the doctor thought it was but wanted us to see this specialist."

Judging by Vanessa's mortified expression I had a feeling that wasn't the point. She wasn't thrilled that Beth was not only sharing but buying into the initial diagnosis.

Quickly, I answered in hopes of defusing the mounting tension and putting them both at ease.

"I'm not a doctor but here in Florida, skin cancers are not uncommon. There are a ton of treatment centers and I know the earlier you catch them, the easier they are to treat or remove." I shifted my gaze back to the rearview mirror. "I'm guessing you've been enjoying the beaches since you moved down, yes?"

Vanessa's face lost its blank stare and she smiled. "Yes, I would go every day if I could."

I looked over at Beth in an effort to poke at her on Vanessa's behalf and also bring her into the conversation.

"You have the same Irish skin that I do. We burn if we leave the kitchen light on too long."

4

Both of the girls laughed. Beth then recalled a long weekend they had spent at Clearwater Beach and how nice it was to get away.

"What did you do for your tenth anniversary?" I asked.

Beth spoke out of the corner of her mouth. "We drove. I drove."

Vanessa laughed and reached up to pat Beth's shoulder. "She did. She was so sweet. We went home to Boston to see our families. They had a big party for us and everyone we knew was there. It was amazing!"

Beth's sour look easily melted away and an expression of fond reflection took its place.

We arrived to the specialist's office and they both thanked me for the ride as they exited my car. Vanessa's anxiety was quickly returning and she half-smiled at me and said, "Wish me luck."

I tried removing some of her concern by referring to her assumed condition of skin cancers as routine. "You'll be fine. This is part of living in Florida, Beach-Girl."

She smiled full-on and they walked toward the office door.

As I drove off, I thought about how lucky they were to have each other. Vanessa's cancer diagnosis obviously filled her with fear. In this time, she needed those she loved and who loved her. She needed Beth and she was right there beside her.

Significant others are, in addition to lovers, friends, allies and partners. They unconditionally band together in unified support of one another. It was uplifting to see love transcend gender and fill the hearts of the two women. They were clearly bonded and above all, true partners.

Chapter Eleven

Not long past my time with Beth and Vanessa I, again, responded to a ride request for two, young women. I arrived to their home in a very upscale neighborhood early on a Thursday evening. As I exited the car, I watched them kiss what I assumed were their boyfriends or husbands, goodbye. Learning from my mistakes, I made it a policy to open the car door for all of my female passengers. The ladies seemed surprised but appreciative of my gesture while the guys they were leaving behind glared down their noses at me.

I sensed that they felt a deep need to inform me, with crossed arms and piercing stares, that the women were their personal property and lived with them in their caves. I inferred that they were ready to pick their knuckles up off of the ground, retrieve their clubs and chase the intruder, me, away. I rolled my eyes at their one-hundred and sixty pound frames and somehow resisted the urge to flex my arms in response. The two guys remained stoic and inhaled the puffiest chest they could hold until I drove off.

In the only other mature moment of the exchange, I held back the urge to wink at them as I left. In hindsight, I *so* should have.

"Where are we off to?" I asked.

Both of the very attractive ladies wore light brown hair down past their shoulders. They appeared to be in their mid-to-late twenties, quiet and a little shy.

"We're going to see Maroon 5." One of them softly responded.

Fully aware of which event center which was hosting the concert, I began the short, mostly interstate, drive without the need of the GPS.

My familiarity with the local radio genres enabled me to choose the station that, on ordinary days, played Maroon 5 at least twice each hour. Surely, on the day of their local concert, they would at least double that and ensure that we would hear a minimum of one Adam Levine fronted tune during our drive.

The second song to play was their current hit, "Animal". The passengers sang along while I did my best Simon Cowell critique, inside my head, of course.

When the song ended, one of them read a text from her phone.

"He's so jealous. It's getting old." She complained to her friend.

"What's his issue, now?" Her friend asked.

There was silence. I looked in the rearview mirror to see the friend looking at me and mouthing, "Oh."

Finding his insecurity humorous, I joined their exchange and said, "Yeah, they both glared a hole in my head when I opened the door for you two. Are they your boyfriends or husbands?"

In unison, they both replied, "Boyfriends."

Still clinging to her phone in frustration of the text, the girl offered, "I am so sorry."

"All good." I replied.

I always wondered what made some guys so insecure where their girlfriends and wives were concerned. I would guess that most guys truly just worry about their girlfriend's or wife's well-being in a not-so-safe world. It's not that they don't trust her; they don't trust the rest of the world.

However, some take it to an extreme. For example, these women's boyfriends glared at me as if I had just been released from prison. If they truly did perceive me as a threat, why didn't they stop me and drive their girlfriends to the concert themselves?

I've seen girls who stick with these kinds of guys and it often doesn't end well. Eventually the guy won't let her out of his sight and she ends up alienating her friends and family.

Just when I thought this girl was one of the weaker ones, she asked me to turn down the radio. I watched as she held the phone to her right ear and projected a very formidable voice.

For the next sixty or so seconds, the girl appeared to speak without breathing and laid down the law to her other half. She very clearly explained to her boyfriend that if his and I quote, "jealous bullshit" didn't stop, that they were done.

The last thing the girl said before hanging up was, "I don't want you to be sorry. I want you to not be jealous."

I dropped them off in front of the event center and made my way back to the interstate. I replayed the girl's lecture on jealousy and insecurity which her boyfriend had endured, with more pleasure than I should have. I'm fairly certain that he will either come around and relax or be kicked to the curb and forced to find someone much weaker.

My impression of the girl was that of a soft-spoken shy pretty, young woman who favored over-bearing tough guys. She proved me wrong when she put him in his place in sixty seconds or less.

Chapter Twelve

Recently, after over four hours of driving, I found myself near the Starbucks that's located in the same plaza as my grocery store and decided to take a short break. As I entered, my eyes immediately caught the sight of the homeless man I had seen several months prior. In my estimation, he didn't look any different. His clothes were still tattered, his face was dirty and he peered through long, straggly, white hair at a newspaper sprawled out in front of him on a small table.

I walked to the counter and asked the barista for a coffee. As she rang up my order, I asked her if she knew anything about the homeless man.

"Mike?" She asked as she glanced over at him. She looked a little suspicious when she asked me, "What do you want to know about him?"

I struggled to choose the most appropriate words but may have failed to appear sensitive. "How did he get...like that?"

The barista smiled knowingly. "What do you think happened?"

My mind brought forth my initial determination of poverty at the hand of an addiction. Not comfortable suggesting such a dark assumption, I shrugged my shoulders, looked over at the man and offered a vague guess.

"Not sure. Wanted by the law?"

She arched an eyebrow as she spoke. "He's wanted alright but not by the police."

I'm pretty sure my head tilted slightly to the left the same way my Lab's head would when he was trying to understand my unfamiliar, human words.

The barista read my confused expression and then looked to the left and then to the right. Her eyes scrutinized our surroundings for privacy. She slowly leaned forward and I felt compelled to do the same.

She spoke low and soft and her eyes never left mine. "He's a lottery winner."

The girl pulled back and fell quiet as if allowing me time to digest the information. She crossed her arms in front of her and raised her chin. She narrowed her eyes with a stare that suggested possession of some esoteric knowledge such as the mysterious intricacies of the Mayan calendar.

Failing to connect the dots, I asked, quietly, "So, why is he homeless?"

The girl rolled her eyes and stepped forward. Another glance from the left and then to the right and then she was ready to continue. "He's in hiding because everyone wants his money. His wife left him and took, like, half of his stuff. He couldn't work because everyone knew he was rich and they said he should let someone else who needed it have his job." She paused and then remembered another reason. "Oh, and I heard some guy robbed his house just so he could hurt himself while he was there and sue him."

"So, he's off the grid?"

Apparently bored with me, she walked away just after answering, "Uh yeah, that's what I said."

I glanced over at the man one more time. Assuming what I was told was true, he lived each day under the weight of the cruel irony that he had become a millionaire, but was unable to live the experience. I considered his commitment to the role as he scrounged coins on the street to support his coffee habit. If he truly was a millionaire, no one would have guessed.

My first impression of the homeless man, like most of my initial assessments, was off the mark. I've learned that it's much more interesting to listen to someone else's story, than it is to assume that I know it.

We all have a story and mine includes a passion to write. Thank you for reading this and helping me to continue to write my story.

I truly hope you enjoyed reading *First Impressions: True Tales from the Road.*

Please check out my short stories, *The 7 Novellas Series* and *The Dead: A True Paranormal Story.* For your enjoyment, I've included the first chapter of *The Dead* below.

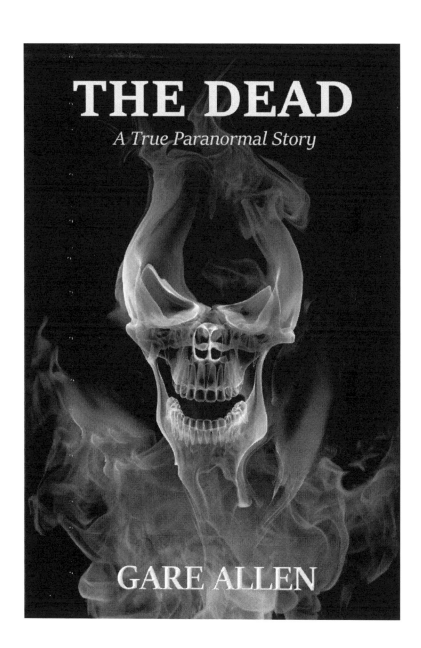

THE DEAD
A True Paranormal Story

GARE ALLEN

The Dead

By

Gare Allen

Preface

I've often been asked if the paranormal activities described in my short stories actually happened to me. My response has always been an honest one.

The stories are all based on actual events or at least what I perceived as real.

If you read the stories, you will see that the main character, Greer, doesn't blindly accept his experiences as real. He investigates them and allows them their due consideration before making a determination. He is more interested in what the events can do to enhance his existence and most importantly, his relationship with Ashley. Whether he accepts the abductions, incarnations, apparitions and projections as reality is really not all that important, as long as he learns from the experiences and grows.

This book explains my early interest and investigation into metaphysical teachings and is also an account of the spiritual and paranormal events that have occurred in my life, thus far.

Chapter One

I was twelve years old when my bed levitated itself.

It was close to ten o'clock on a school night when I decided to go to sleep and was immediately joined by the family dog, Patches.

While attending an elementary school carnival roughly five years earlier, my mother happened upon a box marked "Free Puppies." Inside remained the runt of the litter; small, covered in fleas and with various colored markings, hence the name, Patches. Mom immediately took pity on the pup and we brought her home. From that point forward, the small, mixed-breed dog's quality of life would, dramatically, increase.

As usual, she found a spot at the foot of the bed and curled into a ball.

My bedroom was located at the top of the mauve, shag carpeted stairs.

It was the early 1980's so don't judge.

Mine was the first bedroom at the beginning of a hallway that led to all the other sleep rooms.

I've never fallen asleep quickly, so I was wide awake a few minutes later when the bed suddenly elevated a few inches off the floor.

While suspended in mid-air, it wobbled slightly. I froze in terror, and the next few seconds felt more like minutes.

1

Feelings of severe angst and confusion consumed me. It was similar to when you fly in a plane or take a ride on a roller coaster. It was a helpless sensation, but there weren't any safety mechanisms in place, and this wasn't a carnival ride. I could see Patches lift her head, prompted by the elevated and unstable motion.

After hovering for two to three seconds, the bed dropped hard and fast, back down to the floor. Patches jumped up and yelped a short, startled cry. My limbs shifted on their own, which provided me proof of my recent movement. Desperate to understand the obvious infraction of physics law, my mind frantically searched for a rational explanation. Simultaneously, I worked to hold back a panic attack by taking in deep breaths and slowly exhaling.

As if on cue, my older brother appeared in my open doorway. Having just walked up the stairs on his way to his bedroom, he stopped and asked, "What was that noise?"

Unable to collect my thoughts and formulate a response, while still trying to regulate my breathing, I simply looked at him. I imagined that my eyes were wide open. I must have had a mixture of confusion, disbelief and fright expressed on my face.

Growing up, I think most big brothers find their younger siblings strange and mostly uninteresting. I'm confident his perception was no exception. A look of wide-eyed terror would simply be another "weird little brother" moment and hardly worth the effort of investigation. He flashed me an eye roll, and then disappeared down the hallway. In hindsight, it was doubtful that he would have believed that the thud he heard as he climbed the stairs was actually my bed landing on the floor.

In shock, I remained motionless for another few minutes until the majority of my panic subsided and I finally found the courage to move. I sat up and looked around my small room.

The silence was eerie as I scanned the room for anything out of the ordinary. The closet door was open, and nothing but a filing cabinet and shoes looked back at me. Continuing my investigation, I confirmed that the window remained shut and was locked. That left just one obvious place to look: under the bed.

I leaned over the side of the mattress and allowed my head to hang down so that my view of the small space between the bed frame and the floor was upside down.

The light coming in from the open door provided just enough illumination to see through the dark space. I ran my hand along the carpet. It was cold. One more swipe of my extended arm resulted in my fingertips brushing against a soft piece of fabric. Assuming it was the match to one of my many, lonely socks, I pulled it out from underneath the bed.

I've always had a thing for, what I now refer to as, classic rock: The Beatles, The Who, The Rolling Stones, The Monkees, etc.

A close second musical favorite was heavy metal, in particular, AC/DC, Black Sabbath and Ozzy Osbourne.

Previously, my parents had reluctantly purchased an Ozzy tapestry and fulfilled my Christmas gift request. The tapestry was nothing more than a large handkerchief, adorned with images of Ozzy and his album covers. I would later see them at fairs and carnivals and understand that they were homemade, silkscreened products.

I held the square piece of fabric with both hands and sat up on the edge of my bed. My eyes inspected the tapestry as if I was going to see something on it that I hadn't before. The hallway light streaming through the door was no longer sufficient for my intense scrutiny, so I stood up, took a few steps toward the switch and flipped on the light. The instant illumination filled the room and I gasped at the edges of the kerchief. Each corner displayed an identical tack hole. Remembering that it had been hanging on my pre-teen wall, adjacent to soccer and football posters, I looked at the area above my bed.

Kids have the luxury of still believing in magic, Santa and in my case, a consistent, winning Tampa Bay Buccaneers team. Perhaps it was this naivety that kept me from sprinting from the room, as I stared at the four tacks on the wall that once held up the tapestry.

Nope, there weren't any tears in the corners of the handkerchief. It clearly hadn't been pulled down and I couldn't determine how it found its way off of my wall with the tacks remaining in place, only to be discovered beneath my bed.

After pulling the thumb tacks from the wall, I hung my Ozzy "artwork" back in place. My careful placement utilized the same tack holes in a concerted effort to deter the inevitable rants of my father regarding the insurmountable damage that tacks and push-pins inflict on wood paneling.

Yes, wood paneling. Again…1980's.

Later, in early adulthood as I studied metaphysics, I would recall the specific images on the kerchief. Hazy and, most likely, unlicensed pictures of Ozzy in concert that were undoubtedly taken from magazines, adorned the corners, with random upside-down crosses filling the outer ring. The center boasted a large star that I would later understand to be a pentagram.

For those wondering, the juxtaposition of a satanic bandana as a Christmas present is not lost on me.

The frightening occurrence of my levitating bed opened my mind enough to allow an exploration of metaphysical concepts. In turn, those experiences would provide the storyline for my series of supernatural short stories, *The 7 Novellas Series.*

50687348R00041

Made in the USA
Charleston, SC
05 January 2016